HE TELLS US TO GO

Also by Ian Coffey

Pennies for Heaven (Giving and Christian Discipleship)
(Kingsway 1984)

HE TELLS US TO GO

Evangelism – Sharing Good News in a Divided World

Ian Coffey

HODDER AND STOUGHTON
LONDON   SYDNEY   AUCKLAND   TORONTO

All quotations are taken from the New
International Version of the Bible unless
otherwise stated

ISBN 0 340 39085 9

CONTENTS

INTRODUCTION

In the middle of a busy city, work was coming to an end on a large skyscraper office block. During the construction project it had been noticed that the building was leaning over at an angle. No building is perfectly straight and upright, but this particular office block was tilting to such an extent that experts ruled it as unsafe for use.

Millions of pounds were tied up in the construction and – human nature being what it is – everyone involved looked for someone else to carry the can, and foot the bill. On investigation it was discovered that, in the initial drawings for the foundations of the building, somebody had made a relatively minor mathematical error which had never been picked up. This set off a chain of events in the construction programme resulting in the problem of an office block with a tilt. Because the foundations were wrong the whole building was affected.

Right foundations are essential. Jesus brought that home with the powerful illustration of the wise and foolish builders (Matt 7:24–27). It is not speed or enthusiastic activity that count, but choosing your foundations wisely. Jesus was making the point that only lives built on him can withstand the storms of life and the floods of God's righteous judgement.

We need right foundations for Christian belief and behaviour. We may be active as Christians – but activity for activity's sake is a world apart from doing the works of God. It has been suggested that if the twentieth-century church needed a patron saint, then St Vitus must be the front-runner in the field of candidates!

It is important to stand back at times and examine why, as Christians, we are doing what we are doing. Or, to put it

another way, why we are *not* doing what we should be doing!
With a Bible in one hand, a newspaper in the other and in a
spirit of prayer we need to constantly ask ourselves the
question, 'What does it mean to follow Christ in a changing
world?'

Evangelism is a reflection of God's heart concern for
people. It is not an activity dreamt up by a committee of the
zealous but an expression of the very character of God
himself. It is bound up with his future plans for Planet Earth.
It is indivisibly linked with Christian discipleship and it is
one of the primary reasons the Church exists at all.

Evangelism is an important part of following Christ in a
changing world. But there are two important questions that
need to be faced in order to ensure that we are building upon
good foundations – 'Why?' and 'How?' This brief booklet sets
out some answers to the questions 'Why should we evangelise?' and 'How should we evangelise?' Because of its size it
can do no more than seek to put up some signposts. Others
have written more fully and with greater skill on the roads
down which these signposts point and some of the most
helpful books on the subject of evangelism are listed in the
Appendix.

The old adage contains a degree of truth: 'Those who can –
do. Those who can't – *teach*.' It is with caution that I seek to
mark out some of the foundations for biblical evangelism,
conscious of the danger of lapsing from doing to merely
talking. It was A W Tozer who mourned the turning of
churches from barracks to classrooms; into producing stu-
dents instead of soldiers. The first Christians were not idle
theorists nor were they mindless hyper-activists. They
gained the reputation of having 'turned the world upside
down' with the good news of Jesus (Acts 17:6, RSV).

God grant us another generation of world-shakers.

1 WHAT IS EVANGELISM?

A definition can kill a thing stone dead. Take, as an example, this definition of 'love' from a psychology textbook: 'The cognitive affective state characterised by intrusive and obsessive fantasising concerning reciprocity of amorant feeling by the object of the amorance.' Try explaining that to a young couple deeply in love!

But definitions are important because they help us to discover what something means. There is always the danger, in the Christian faith, of making into a science what God actually intended as an art form. We can become lost in the study of the mechanics so that we miss the beauty of the mystery.

With these cautions in mind we need to face three questions and come up with some definitions.

WHAT IS EVANGELISM?

Evangelism, put simply, is telling the good news of Jesus Christ. It has, as its object, the bringing of people to personal faith in God, through Jesus Christ, so that they may become his effective disciples serving him in his world and in his church.

The message in evangelism is God's message. The person engaging in evangelism is entrusted with that message in the same way that an ambassador conveys the views of his king or, as in bygone years, a town crier shouted out the proclamation he had been given.

The responsibility to evangelise belongs to every Christian disciple as an individual as well as to the church as a whole.

The task of making Christ known is part of being salt and light in a decaying and darkening world.

In 1974, Christians from all over the world met in the historic International Congress on World Evangelization in Lausanne, Switzerland. Those who attended recognised both the challenges and opportunities that faced the world church in the closing quarter of the twentieth century. They drafted and agreed what has become known as the Lausanne Covenant. Part of that Covenant deals with the meaning of evangelism:

> To evangelise is to spread the good news that Jesus Christ died for our sins and was raised from the dead according to the Scriptures, and that as the reigning Lord he now offers the forgiveness of sins and the liberating gift of the Spirit to all who repent and believe. Our Christian presence in the world is indispensable to evangelism, and so is that kind of dialogue whose purpose is to listen sensitively in order to understand. But evangelism itself is the proclamation of the historical, biblical Christ as Savior and Lord, with a view to persuading people to come to him personally and so be reconciled to God. In issuing the Gospel invitation we have no liberty to conceal the cost of discipleship. Jesus still calls all who would follow him to deny themselves, take up their cross, and identify themselves with his new community. The results of evangelism include obedience to Christ, incorporation into his church and responsible service in the world.
>
> (Lausanne Covenant Paragraph 4 in J R W Stott *The Lausanne Covenant: An Exposition and Commentary*, (World-wide Publications 1975)

But words without actions can be meaningless. They both went inextricably together in the ministry of Jesus. Quoting the familiar words of Isaiah the prophet, Jesus preached in the synagogue of his home town in Nazareth:

> The Spirit of the Lord is on me, because he has anointed me to preach good news to the poor. He has sent me to proclaim freedom for the prisoners and recovery of sight for the blind, to release the oppressed, to proclaim the year of the Lord's favour.
> (Luke 4:18–19)

He claimed the fulfilment of Isaiah's prophecy in himself and then went about demonstrating it by proclamation and action. He meant what he said. The late David Watson wrote:

> It was never the bare proclamation of words. Always it was words set in action: not just 'signs and wonders', of course, but numerous examples of the love and care and compassion of the one who had come to bring good news . . . Here was powerful evangelism, not only because of the faithful announcement of God's Kingdom, but also because of the good deeds that accompanied the good words.
> (David Watson *I Believe in Evangelism* (Hodder and Stoughton 1974) p 28–9)

Christ's disciples today are called to tread the same path and, in our evangelism as well as every aspect of our life, 'Whoever claims to live in him must walk as Jesus did' (1 John 2:6).

WHAT IS AN EVANGELICAL CHRISTIAN?

'Evangelicals are among the fastest-growing branches of Christianity in our time,' writes Waldron Scott, the President of the American Leprosy Mission (Robin Keele, (ed) *Christianity: A World Faith* (Lion Publishing 1985) p 107). They make up more than one in six of the worldwide Christian population and best estimates are of nearly 270 million in 1985. Within the term 'evangelical' there are many

sub-groups and individual Christians who belong to denominations which are themselves not evangelical.

Evangelicals do not all share exactly the same beliefs, but,
broadly speaking, there are three areas of common ground:

The Bible

'Evangelicals are Bible people . . .' declared John Stott at the
1977 National Evangelical Anglican Congress. They view
the Bible as the inspired word of God and believe that
scripture has supreme authority over the church in all
matters of faith and practice. What matters is what the Bible
says about the church rather than what the church thinks
about the Bible.

The new birth

Evangelicals take their title from the word *evangel*, which
means good news, or gospel. They focus on the biblical call
for a personal relationship with God through faith in Jesus
Christ. This is made possible only by the work of the Holy
Spirit who alone can regenerate a person. Being *born again*,
although sometimes an abused term, is a biblical picture
given by Jesus himself to describe the Christian conversion
experience (See John 3:3–8).

World mission

Historically, evangelicals have always had a strong commitment to mission. Their view of the Bible and the gospel has
driven them to a global vision. 'The world is my parish',
explained John Wesley, and that accurately summarises a
true evangelical outlook. Not that evangelicals have seen
people as merely souls that need saving. The history of the
Christian church would be poorer without the zeal of evange-

licals such as Wilberforce, Booth, Shaftesbury, Müller, Barnardo and the like.

WHY IS EVANGELISM IMPORTANT?

The preacher looked earnestly over the pulpit: 'But isn't that just modal monarchianism in another guise? I hear you ask.' The congregation stared back in blank amazement. The question was not even understood let alone asked.

We live in an age of questions. Sadly, as Christians, we sometimes find ourselves answering the questions that no one is asking. It is all too easy to become preoccupied with peripheral issues whilst leaving the world's questions unanswered. Matters such as authority, church structures, forms of worship and theological nuances may make for stimulating in-house discussions but they can distract us from our primary task as Christians. Michael Green has pointed out: 'The Christians of New Testament days saw dynamic worship, together with bold and imaginative evangelism, as the twin purposes for which the church existed. They put first things first. With us, first things often come last' (Michael Green *Evangelism Now and Then* (IVP) 1979) p 9).

All the indications show that time is short. World population now doubles every thirty years, producing new generations who need to hear the message of Jesus Christ. The threat of a nuclear holocaust looms large and the needs of the poor, the underprivileged and the oppressed are beamed into our living rooms through the television screen. The rising tide of secularism is a sign of the gradual erosion of our western society. The world stands at a crossroads. The poor, the prisoners, the blind, the oppressed and the great unloved still need good news in words and actions.

A NEW COMMITMENT

Evangelical Christians need to make a renewed commitment to evangelism for a number of reasons.

* Biblical foundations the Bible makes it clear that God is committed to world evangelisation. He is the prime mover in evangelism.

* Historical heritage our spiritual forefathers translated their belief in the Bible, the gospel and the needs of the world into radical action.

* Concern for the church the worldwide church needs to get back to basics. Biblical evangelism is essential for every church if it is to grow spiritually healthy. As well as telling fellow Christians to get involved in evangelism we need to be involved ourselves. Historical heritage is meaningless unless we stay true to its principles. Exhortation and example belong together.

* Responsibility to this generation Only one life – it will soon be past, Only what's done for Jesus will last.

It may sound trite but it is true! We carry the responsibility for communicating Christ in today's world in language and ideas that people can understand. It is a heavy responsibility and one that we cannot escape.

* Commitment to Jesus Christ His command to 'go and make disciples of all nations' (Matt 28:19) is unalterable. Our need to obey it as part of our discipleship is undeniable.

As evangelicals, we have the reputation for being conservative in our theology, but the need of the hour – for the world at the crossroads – is for us to become radical in our discipleship and unafraid to harness new methods. Wesley and his horse, Booth with his band and Blessitt and his cross are striking examples of what happens when radical discipleship and imaginative thinking meet. Christian innovators may not always win friends, but they influence a lot of people.

2 EVANGELISM AND THE BIBLE

An inventor was proudly showing his latest creation to a close friend. The machine was an amazing assortment of wires, dials, levers and switches. 'Very impressive,' the friend remarked, 'but what exactly does it *do*?' The inventor looked puzzled. '*Do*? Well, er, actually it doesn't *do* anything – but doesn't it do it beautifully?'

We can easily find ourselves trapped in a helter-skelter of activity and a merry-go-round of meetings without ever stepping back and considering what we are doing and why we are doing it. Unless we first take time to think through our motivation and aims, even engaging in evangelism can prove to be a frenetic waste of spiritual energy. Jim Graham has written of some timely advice he once received, 'Make sure that you don't substitute busyness for blessedness, because busyness can often lead to barrenness of spirit' (Jim Graham *Prayer* (Scripture Union 1985) p 23). That is why, as a matter of priority, we need to consider what the Bible has to say about evangelism. We shall take a brief look at:

* What the Bible teaches us about the character of God.
* The message that the first Christians preached, the motives that inspired them and the methods that they used.
* God's marching orders for his church in every generation.

THE DOCTRINE OF GOD

Although the word 'trinity' does not appear anywhere in the Bible, the truth of God in three persons is implicit throughout its pages. God – the Father, the Son and the Spirit: each member of the trinity – is bound up with mission.

God is a missionary. From Genesis to Revelation the truth stands out that God is always concerned to reveal himself to those who do not already know him. Indeed, God seems caught up in the business of self-disclosure. In the early chapters of Genesis we read of God revealing himself to Abraham with the promise to bless him and his family. But this promise has a global dimension, 'all peoples on earth will be blessed through you' (Gen 12:3).

The nature and heart of God the Father is revealed in a remarkable passage in the gospels, where Luke groups together the three 'lost' parables. Jesus speaks of a man who lost a sheep, a woman who lost a coin and a father who lost a son. The shepherd scoured the hillsides, the woman swept her house and the father surveyed the horizon. Perhaps few of the parables created as much shock as did the story of the father running to meet his returning son. Human nature cried out for anything but the welcome he received. But the nature of God is *grace* – giving that which no one deserves. 'God is like that!' declared Jesus, and the crowd listened, stunned into silence. In Luke 15, we have our finger on the pulse of God.

Jesus, the Son, sent out his disciples to preach the good news of the arrival of the king and his kingdom. First the twelve and later the seventy were sent (Matt 10:1–15; Luke 10:1–12). Their commission was not only to proclaim the kingdom but also to demonstrate its authority, invested in them through Jesus, by healing the sick and exorcising the demonised. Although the commission was at first limited 'to the lost sheep of Israel' it was later widened to include 'all nations'. In one of the gospel summaries of his mission Jesus said 'For the Son of Man came to seek and to save what was lost' (Luke 19:10). Like Father, like Son.

The Holy Spirit has been rightly described as the 'missionary Spirit' and Pentecost as a 'missionary event'. The promise of his coming reveals something of the purpose of his coming: Jesus predicted, 'But you will receive power when the Holy Spirit comes on you; and you will be my witnesses in Jerusalem, and in all Judea and Samaria, and to the ends of the earth' (Acts 1:8). Luke, who wrote the book of Acts in addition to his own gospel, reports the results of the work of the missionary Spirit. One New Testament scholar describes Acts in these terms: 'It is a story of the minute but mighty mustard seed; it is the narrative of the Holy Spirit championing and vindicating the cause of Christ in such a way that prison-bars go down like clay before the divine decree . . .' (C F D Moule *The Birth of the New Testament* (A and C Black 1978) p 92).

The Holy Spirit was actively involved in the ministry of Jesus. John the Baptist prophesied that the coming Messiah would baptise people in the Holy Spirit (Mark 1:8). Jesus declared that a person could not see or enter the kingdom without the supernatural work of the Spirit (John 3:3,5). Jesus promised that the Spirit would be sent after he had returned to heaven and that his special work would include: guiding Jesus' disciples into all truth; glorifying Jesus by making his will known to his followers; convicting the world of sin, righteousness and judgement (John 16:5–16). Jesus made the link quite clear; before his disciples could effectively witness about him, they needed the power of the Holy Spirit in them and upon them (Acts 1:8).

In the trinitarian doctrine of God we find a trinitarian basis for evangelism. Father, Son and Spirit are all engaged in mission. 'The God who is there' revealed himself to Moses, the refugee royal, through a burning bush in a desert; to a devastated Job in the anguish of suffering; to a Roman centurion one hot afternoon through a vision; to a teenage girl called Mary with the announcement of a miraculous pregnancy and to a self-righteous Pharisee named Saul through a blinding light on the road to Damascus. 'He is there; and he is not silent', wrote Francis Shaeffer.

The call to evangelise, which applies to every Christian, is bound up in the very nature and character of God himself.

THE FIRST CHRISTIANS

A detailed study of the New Testament reveals not only the priority that the first Christians gave to evangelism but also the distinct note of urgency that they sounded as they set about the task of making Christ known to the world. They saw as their target group people everywhere and they understood that their time-scale was short. They lived in the expectation that Jesus would return to earth very soon and his words rang in their ears, 'As long as it is day, we must do the work of him who sent me. Night is coming, when no-one can work' (John 9:4).

Donald Guthrie has pointed out:

> The early church did not work itself up into an evangelistic community. It inherited a command from the risen Christ which it could not ignore. He did not give much indication on church organization, but he left in no doubt what the main aims of the community of his followers was to be. The idea of a closed, inward-looking community finds no support from his teaching. The message entrusted to his disciples was intended for all the world.
> (Donald Guthrie *New Testament Theology* (IVP 1981) p 716)

Their message

The exact content of the early church's preaching about Jesus has been a subject of much study and debate amongst New Testament scholars for a number of decades. In 1936,

Professor C H Dodd of Cambridge University published his now famous book entitled *The Apostolic Preaching and its Developments*. Since its publication this small book has caused a considerable amount of ink to be spilt by theologians.

Dodd claimed that the writers of the New Testament drew a clear distinction between preaching (for which the Greek noun is *kerygma*) and teaching (Greek, *didachē*). *Teaching*, said Dodd, concentrated mainly on ethical instructions, with some well argued reasons for belief for those interested in Christianity but not yet convinced, and the teaching of theological doctrine. *Preaching*, on the other hand, focused on the public proclamation of Christianity to the non-Christian world. Teaching was for insiders and preaching for outsiders, according to Dodd. He believed that much of the preaching in the churches of his day would not have been regarded by the early Christians as authentic preaching – it was more teaching for those already established in the faith.

Dodd set out to discover the actual content of the gospel which was preached by the first Christians to their world, and he put forward his own analysis (C H Dodd *The Apostolic Preaching and its Developments* (Hodder and Stoughton, 1972) p 21–23).

The theologians have debated Dodd's conclusions and by no means do they all agree! Michael Green, in his classic study *Evangelism in the Early Church* (Hodder and Stoughton 1970), summarises the main arguments superbly but rejects Dodd's approach as being too much like a straitjacket. Certainly, there was a core message which the first Christians preached, most scholars would agree, but, undoubtedly, there was a greater degree of flexibility in how that message was presented than Dodd permits. That core message was ultimately drawn together in the apostles' creed.

But C H Dodd has done an immense service to the church by forcing us to think through the issue of what the first Christians preached as their gospel. They moved in a cosmopolitan world confronting Jews and Gentiles with the mes-

sage of Jesus, recognising that language, religious beliefs,
thought-forms, culture and tradition varied drastically from
community to community. The first Christians became skil-
led at translating their message without devaluing its content.

From examining the book of Acts and the accounts of
evangelistic preaching it contains we can discover, in sketch
outline, something of the content of that core message.

They centred on Jesus

From Peter's first evangelistic address on the day of Pentecost (Acts 2:14–39) to the last glimpse we have of Paul
conducting house-meetings in Rome (Acts 28:30–31) the
message is centred on the activity of God in the life of Jesus of
Nazareth. Philip, confronted with an enquiring African on a
desert road, 'told him the good news about Jesus' (Acts 8:35).
Stephen, on trial for his life before the Jewish court of the
Sanhedrin preached about Jesus as 'the Righteous One' long
promised by the God of the Jews (Acts 7:52); and the
husband and wife team of Aquila and Priscilla helped the
enthusiastic Apollos to understand the gospel more ade-
quately with the result that soon he 'vigorously refuted the
Jews in public debate, proving from the Scriptures that Jesus
was the Christ (or Messiah)' (Acts 18:28). The very charges
laid against the first Christians prove the centrality of Jesus
in their message; 'They are all defying Caesar's decrees,
saying that there is another king, one called Jesus' (Acts
17:7).

The core message of the gospel declared that Jesus of
Nazareth was the central figure. His person, mighty acts,
atoning death on the cross, resurrection, ascension into
heaven and expected personal return to earth were proclaimed. This was all set in the context of the promises of God
that the Messiah would one day come. To Jewish audiences

great pains were taken to prove the fulfilment in Jesus of the Old Testament passages referring to the Messiah. Even to the Gentiles, who were largely ignorant of the Jewish scriptures, it was pointed out that it was the God of all creation who had acted in Jesus. The outpouring of the Holy Spirit upon ordinary men and women was seen as evidence of the resurrection and ascension of Jesus (Acts 2:32–33).

The first Christians unambiguously proclaimed God's gift of salvation, made available through Jesus. There were two elements to this gift:

i) Forgiveness of sin
ii) Receiving the Holy Spirit

Peter declared the gift to the puzzled crowd in Jerusalem with these words: 'Repent and be baptised, every one of you, in the name of Jesus Christ so that your sins may be forgiven. And you will receive the gift of the Holy Spirit. The promise is for you and your children and for all who are far off – for all whom the Lord our God will call' (Acts 2:38–39).

When called to give an account of his activities before the Jewish rulers, Peter makes the emphatic and exclusive claim: 'Salvation is found in no-one else, for there is no other name under heaven given to men by which we must be saved' (Acts 4:12). For the first Christians, Jesus *was* the good news.

They concentrated on key truths

The early Christians focused their preaching on certain key truths concerning Jesus. Their approach varied depending on the audience and circumstances but from the accounts in Acts of their evangelism, as well as the New Testament letters, we can recognise some of the themes they repeated.

Jesus is the Messiah

The Jews expected God's Messiah to come. The Old Testament promised a deliverer would arise from the line of David. The first Christians pointed to the fulfilment of the prophecies in the person of Jesus of Nazareth (Acts 7:52; 13:23).

The cross

The writers of the New Testament deal with the crucifixion of Jesus as a matter of fact. But neither they nor the first Christian preachers seemed content to leave it there. The cross *was* a fact – but it held deep meaning. Many men had been crucified; from runaway slaves to rebels against Roman rule.

In the brutal days of the first century, sadly, there was nothing unusual about a man on a cross. But what gave the death of Jesus great significance was, firstly, the person who died. He was none less than, in Paul's words, 'the Son of God, who loved me and gave himself for me' (Gal 2:20). Secondly, the first Christians emphasised what Jesus accomplished through his death. Great words, pregnant with meaning, are used in the New Testament to convey the truth that Jesus died as our substitute and sin-bearer. Words such as redemption (to buy back or pay a ransom), covenant (a legal agreement), propitiation (conveying the idea of covering sin and turning away God's righteous anger), reconciliation (the bringing together of estranged parties) and justification (a legal term where a person is declared 'not guilty' but righteous) are taken up and used to describe the meaning of the death of Jesus.

Peter, who was probably an eyewitness outside Jerusalem on the first Good Friday, conveys the meaning of the death of Jesus when he writes, 'He himself bore our sins in his body on the tree, so that we might die to sin and live for righteousness; by his wounds you have been healed' (1 Pet 2:24).

The resurrection

Tracing the evangelistic preaching in Acts we find that the
resurrection of Jesus is the most repeated theme. It is stated
as a fact of history by those who were there; 'God has raised
this Jesus to life, and we are all witnesses of the fact' (Acts
2:32). But, once again, it is the meaning as well as the fact
that the early Christians emphasise. God raised Jesus up in
fulfilment of the Old Testament prophecies (Acts 2:24–28,
26:22–23) and it was his vindication of his Son.

It is important to notice that the resurrection of Jesus is so
clearly emphasised particularly as, throughout church history, there have been those who have suggested that Jesus'
rising again must be understood symbolically rather than
literally. It was not a vague idea that, in spite of death, the
spirit of Jesus lived on that motivated the first Christians:
'But God raised him from the dead, and for many days he
was seen by those who had travelled with him from Galilee to
Jerusalem. They are now his witnesses to our people' (Acts
13:30–31).

The kingdom of God

Jesus, as the king, had come proclaiming the arrival of his
kingdom (Mark 1:14–15). The first Christians, as citizens of
this new kingdom, enthusiastically proclaimed the rule and
reign of God through Jesus. The good news is called 'the
gospel of the kingdom' (Matt 4:23; 24:14, RSV) and Luke,
who wrote the book of Acts, summarises Paul's three months
of preaching in the synagogue at Ephesus by saying he was
'arguing persuasively about the kingdom of God' (Acts 19:8).

In calling people to repentance and faith, the early Christians called them to acknowledge the lordship of Jesus and the
authority of his kingdom's rule.

The judgement to come

Paul faced the sceptical philosophers and debaters of Athens with a plain, uncomfortable truth about God, 'he has set a day when he will judge the world with justice by the man he has appointed' (Acts 17:31). The early Christian evangelists made no apology in spelling out people's accountability to the God who created them.

The judgement to come was a central theme of the ministry of Jesus. He spoke of coming to seek and save lost people (Luke 19:10) and giving his life as a ransom (Matt 20:28). The implications were clear, people were lost and at the same time imprisoned. Jesus taught about heaven and he also talked about hell. He spoke of the separation of the righteous and the unrighteous at the end of this age. For the righteous there would be eternal life and for the unrighteous eternal punishment (Matt 25:46). Strong, uncomfortable words and if they had come from the lips of anyone other than Jesus we would find them even harder to believe.

The doctrine of hell is difficult but unavoidable if we take the Bible seriously, and the first Christians stressed the urgency of their message in the light of the approaching judgement. In Peter's sermon at the home of the Roman centurion Cornelius he declared, concerning Jesus, 'He commanded us to preach to the people and to testify that he is the one whom God has appointed as judge of the living and the dead' (Acts 10:42).

They called for a response

The early Christians preached for a verdict. They called people not merely to listen to the message about Jesus, but to respond with a conscious, moral choice of the will. That response embraced three activities:

Repentance

The good news about Jesus, they claimed, demanded a radical break with the past way of living. Repentance means a change of mind, a change of heart and a change of direction. Forgiveness was available on the basis of the death of Jesus on the cross on man's behalf. But God, who will one day judge the world with justice, now 'commands all people everywhere to repent' and receive his offer of forgiveness and the Holy Spirit (Acts 17:30).

Faith

Paul spoke of this second element of response to God when he reminded the elders of the church at Ephesus of his evangelistic work in their city, 'I have declared to both Jews and Greeks that they must turn to God in repentance and have faith in our Lord Jesus' (Acts 20:21). In order to receive God's forgiveness and his Spirit, a person must believe in Jesus, as Peter explained to Cornelius and his family: 'All the prophets testify about him that everyone who believes in him receives forgiveness of sins through his name' (Acts 10:43).

The first preachers declared that a person cannot live the Christian life until he has trusted in Christ. Saving faith is exercised by, literally, trusting 'on to Christ' and the Christian life is lived by remaining 'in Christ'. Faith, in the New Testament, is seen not only in terms of belief but also obedience. An individual's faith is demonstrated in the way that he lives as well as by the things he says (James 2:14–17; Rom 1:5).

Baptism and discipleship

Repentance and faith are described in Acts in terms of 'turning'. Repentance is turning *from* sin and faith is turning *to* Christ. Baptism and the life of discipleship were seen as outward demonstrations of true conversion. Baptism in water was, for the early church, a public act of identification for a follower of Jesus. Richly symbolic, it signified the burying of the 'old life' and the raising from the grave of the 'new life' in Christ. As Jesus was buried and raised by God's power in the resurrection, so an individual, through faith in him, could bury the past and be raised to a new level of living.

The New Testament is full of teaching on the meaning of baptism. For the new Christian it was the badge of discipleship; the outward demonstration of an inward change. It symbolised the washing away of the stain and guilt of sin, entering into the new covenant community and being united with Christ.

The life of discipleship was included in the response to the gospel. Luke gives us a tantalisingly brief glimpse of the first Christian church at Jerusalem in its early days (Acts 2:42 47). These new Christians 'devoted themselves' to certain things as an expression of their commitment to Christ. Biblical teaching, real fellowship, remembering Christ in the breaking of bread and vital intercessory prayer were obviously high priorities. There was practical concern for the needs of others in the community who had needs, spontaneous generosity and joyful worship. And they were no isolated, inward-looking group as the daily influx of new believers demonstrates. The call to respond to God in repentance and faith may have been personal but it was no private thing. People were called to identify with Christ in his church, at times enjoying the favour and approval of non-believers, but soon that became a costly identification involving suffering and even death.

The good news about Jesus demanded a response, and, without hesitating, the first Christians spelt it out to their hearers by language and lifestyle.

Their motivation

What motivated the early church in their worldwide missionary zeal? The short answer is found not in a principle but a
person – the Holy Spirit. He is the prime mover in evangelism. Jesus had promised his disciples that they would receive
power to become witnesses 'when the Holy Spirit comes on
you' (Acts 1:8) and that same Spirit would thrust them out
into the ends of the earth. As D L Moody said, 'There is not a
better evangelist in the world than the Holy Spirit.'

From the various New Testament letters we gain an
insight into the theological reasons that lay behind the early
Christians' evangelism. They were not out for prestige,
money or power. In fact, many of the first preachers suffered
imprisonment, torture and death. What drove them on with
such selfless commitment to the spreading of the gospel?

They had a sense of gratitude

The first Christians did not evangelise because it was socially
responsible or advisable to do so, but out of their own
experience of God's grace received through Jesus. One of the
results of being justified by faith, writes Paul, is that 'God has
poured out his love into our hearts by the Holy Spirit, whom
he has given us' (Rom 5:5). It is in the light of God's mercy,
he teaches, that Christians are to offer themselves as 'living
sacrifices' as an act of worship (Rom 12:1). Grace makes you
grateful, and that motivated the new believers to demonstrate their gratitude.

They had a sense of accountability

The leaders of the early Christian church had a view of the
future that deeply affected their lives in the present. They

believed fervently in the personal return of Jesus Christ to the world. Although the gospel had removed the fear of judgement they believed they were accountable for the responsibilities left to them. This is what Paul had in mind when he explains to the church in Corinth the basis of his ministry: 'Since, then, we know what it is to fear the Lord, we try to persuade men' (2 Cor 5:11). This was no abject terror or superstitious fear, as Paul goes on to explain: 'For Christ's love compels us' (2 Cor 5:14). It was this sense of being accountable to God that motivated and inspired them.

They had a sense of discovery

It was Archimedes, the story goes, who having made his great discovery ran naked into the street from his bath crying 'Eureka!' ('I have found it!') There was a sense of 'Eureka' about the evangelism of the early church. In Jesus they had found the key to the mystery of the universe. The philosophers and the religious leaders of their world had pondered and probed the meaning of life, its origins and goal. The first Christians proclaimed that 'Christ (is) the power of God and the wisdom of God' (1 Cor 1:24) and in him 'are hidden all the treasures of wisdom and knowledge' (Col 2:3).

It has been said that a man with an experience is never at the mercy of a man with an argument and the early church leaders based their fearless claims on the evidence they themselves had experienced.

Three word-groups in the Greek language are used in the New Testament to describe the proclamation of the gospel: *kerussein* which conveys the idea 'to proclaim' like a herald or town crier;
euaggelizesthai which means 'to tell good news';
marturein which means 'to bear witness'.

This last word, *marturein*, is particularly interesting. It is primarily a legal term used to denote witnesses to facts and

events and also truths vouched for. In both cases, the
personal involvement and assurance of the person making
the witness was an important element. The sense of bearing
witness to facts comes through strongly in the Acts sermons
(Acts 2:32; 3:15; 5:32; 10:39) as well as in the New Testament
letters (1 John 1:1; 2 Pet 1:16). We have gained from *marturein*
the English word 'martyr' – a person who dies for what he
believes. Witness became synonymous with martyrdom. The
early Christians staked their lives on what they knew to be
the truth.

They had a sense of concern

The first Christians preached that Jesus Christ had come to
seek and to save the lost. This was the supreme purpose of the
incarnation and the believing community have reflected that
same passionate concern for people. Their love for people
was real. William Barclay has written, '*The basis of the
Christian ethic is concern* . . . The Gospels have a word for this
attitude of concern. They call it love' (William Barclay *Ethics
in a Permissive Society* (Fontana 1977) p 31, 33).

   Their gospel had not only a personal application but also
social implications. It addressed the racial divisions in society (Jew and Greek), the sexual discrimination (male and
female) and the social inequalities (slave and free) proclaiming that God, in Jesus, had found a new community based on
the truth that 'you are all one in Christ Jesus' (Gal 3:28).
Their practical love in the care of the widows in Jerusalem
(Acts 6:1–4) and the provision of aid to an impoverished
group of believers (1 Cor 16:1–3; 2 Cor 9:1–5) demonstrates
that they perceived that the gospel was not merely concerned
with men's souls but their whole being.

They had a sense of responsibility

Paul sums this up in his letter to the church at Rome as he shares his heartfelt burden for his own people, the Israelites: 'How, then, can they call on the one they have not believed in? And how can they believe in the one of whom they have not heard? And how can they hear without someone preaching to them? And how can they preach unless they are sent?' (Rom 10:14–15).

The feeling of urgency which grips the heart from the pages of the New Testament stems from the sense of responsibility felt by the first believers to share the good news of Jesus with those who had not heard, and to do so with speed because of the brevity of time available. It is worth pointing out that history indicates that the church has always been most effective in evangelism when it has held a strong view of the return of Christ. Deadlines always serve to sharpen vision.

Their methods

The early church was faced with a multifaith, multinational and multicultural world on its doorstep. Helpful studies have been written contrasting the varieties of approach employed in meeting these demands. In Jewish settings, the first Christians used the many scattered synagogues as a starting-point for their evangelism and relied heavily on the Old Testament scriptures to back up the content of their message. The hiring of a lecture theatre in Ephesus and Paul's knowledge of Greek poetry, which he quotes in his Athenian sermon, reveals that a good deal of thought went into the strategy for reaching the Gentiles. Was the strategist human or divine? The answer is probably a bit of both. Undoubtedly the first Christian missionaries thought through their approach carefully but it is important that the first major organised evangelistic enterprise was initiated by God (Acts 13: 1–5).

What methods did the early Christians employ to communicate the good news about Jesus Christ? The fact that for the first 150 years or so churches had no buildings, as such, must have influenced their strategy in evangelism. *Preaching* played a central part in their proclamation of Jesus. Preaching in synagogues (Acts 13:13–43), in the open air (Acts 8:5) and in secular centres (Acts 17:19). The *use of the home* for teaching and preaching is prevalent. One of the most important factors in the spreading of the gospel was the use of the home. In Acts we read of homes being used in Thessalonica (17:7), Corinth (18:7), Caesarea (10:25), Philippi (16:34), and John Mark's mother's home became the centre for the Jerusalem church (12:12). There is also a strong emphasis on *personal evangelism*, with Philip and the Ethiopian royal official being one of the most striking examples (Acts 8:26–39). Court appearances were seized upon as opportunities to testify to Jesus 26:1–29, and there is evidence that Paul, whilst in prison, lost no time in sharing his faith with his guards (Philippians 1:13; 4:22)!

Literature was another method used in evangelism. The first Christians invented a whole new literary form – the gospel. The gospel writers had as their main aim evangelism as they set out the facts about Jesus.

Their use of the *Old Testament scriptures* and their dependence upon God through *prayer* are two important factors in reaching an understanding of how the first believers set about the task of making Christ known.

The historians all seem to agree that Christianity began essentially as a lay movement. Much lies behind the simple statement: 'Those who had been scattered preached the word wherever they went' (Acts 8:4). As one historian has written: 'we cannot hesitate to believe that the great mission of Christianity was in reality accomplished by means of informal missionaries'.

Some have gone as far as to suggest that it is dubious from Acts if the early church even perceived a separate group called 'evangelists'. Everyone was called to the task of spreading the good news. It is challenging to note, in Michael Green's words, 'the little man . . . was the prime agent in mission.' (Michael Green *Evangelism in the Early Church* (Highland Books 1984), p 208)

The first Christians used every method at their disposal to share their faith in Jesus Christ. No wonder it has been noted that '. . . evangelism is absolutely inseparable from the life of the Church (when it is alive) . . .' (Moule *The Birth of the New Testament* p 3).

THE MISSION OF THE CHURCH

Confusion sometimes arises over the words 'mission' and 'evangelism'. In fact, they are almost indivisibly entwined. If there is a distinction to be made (and it must be made with great care) it would be to say that *mission* describes the overall ministry of the church in the world whereas *evangelism* more particularly denotes the activity of making known the good news of Jesus. Each is involved in the other. Bishop Leslie Newbigin of India once described mission as 'the concern that in places where there are no Christians there should be Christians'. Similarly, evangelism that addresses the spiritual condition of people solely, without regard to their physical, mental and moral wellbeing, cannot truly represent the love of Christ.

How did the first Christians perceive their mission? What instructions did Jesus leave them in order to carry on the work of the kingdom? The great commission must be a starting-point:

Jesus came to them and said, 'All authority in heaven and on earth has been given to me. Therefore go and make disciples of all nations, baptising them in the name of the Father and of the Son and of the Holy Spirit, and teaching them to obey everything I have commanded you. And surely I will be with you always, to the very end of the age.' (Matt 28:18–20)

Jesus clearly conceived his disciples forming a community (the church) but he gave very little instruction about its structures. But he did give explicit instructions about its activities. They were called to reproduce. Jesus laid out the ground rules:

* The authority is his by right. The mission of the church is no man-centred activity.
* The commission is universal: all nations are to be reached.
* Making disciples is the goal.
* Baptism is the badge of discipleship.
* Disciples are to be taught faithfully the content of Jesus' teaching.
* The promise of the presence of Jesus is assured to the end of the age.

Undoubtedly, the early church saw that their mission included teaching new converts and establishing local churches under responsible leadership. We have already pointed out there was a strong social dimension in their understanding of the gospel about a God who cares. When it came to the care of widows in the Jerusalem church, the men who were set aside specifically for this task of service received the laying on of hands with the same sense of divine ordination that the apostles had in their own ministries (Acts 6:6). But central to the task of mission was evangelism. In Acts we do not find a church wrestling with priorities. Evangelism, teaching, planting churches, pastoral care and social action seem interwoven. All that they did was done in the name of Jesus, through the power of the Spirit sent by Jesus and with a conscious commitment to the commission of the risen Jesus.

The great Scottish theologian, James Denney, once wrote, 'I have not the slightest interest in a theology which does not help us to evangelize.' He would have felt at home amongst friends with the first Christians.

3   EVANGELISM IN TODAY'S MARKETPLACE

The Christian Church is never stronger or more healthy than when it is fully committed to the work of evangelism. Evangelism is the lifeblood of the church. History gives many examples of periods when the church was in decline, suffering from a loss of direction, and then God moved through the life of an individual or a group of people. A study of the history of great revivals reveals that a common factor is a renewed concern amongst God's people for those outside of Christ.

Revivals and great evangelistic movements cannot be seen as recruitment exercises for the church with little reference to basic problems in society. Jonathan Edwards was a man used by God in the Great Awakening in America in the eighteenth century. The Spirit of God began to do an extraordinary work in a church which he pastored in Northampton, Massachusetts. That work drastically affected the whole town and spread – like a fire – to surrounding communities. Edwards writes of what happened:

> There was scarcely a single person in the town, old or young, left unconcerned about the great things of the eternal world . . . the town seemed to be full of the presence of God: it was never so full of *love*, nor of *joy*, and yet so full of distress, as it was then. There were remarkable tokens of God's presence in almost every house.
> (Jonathan Edwards *A Faithful Narrative of the Surprising Work of God* in *The Works of Jonathan Edwards* (Banner of Truth 1974) p 348)

George Whitefield and the Wesley brothers, John and Charles, were greatly used by God in the Evangelical Awakening in Britain at around the same time. There is no question that thousands were brought into the kingdom of God, many Christians were renewed and church structures changed, as witnessed by the emergence of the Methodist movement. Society as a whole was affected. The revival encouraged a passion for justice; prison reform, the needs of the poor and the movement for the abolition of slavery were high on the priorities list. Just four days before his death, John Wesley wrote to the anti-slavery campaigner William Wilberforce, 'go on, in the name of God, and in the power of his might, till every American slavery (the vilest that ever saw the sun) shall vanish away before it . . .' As one historian has described it, 'The Evangelical Revival made England aware of its social obligations'; and another writes: 'Wesley touched a tender spot on the contemporary conscience . . .'

Church history provides many further examples of how the good news of the Christian gospel, when believed and applied, can make a radical difference within society. Biblical evangelism is not just concerned with men's souls, but the salvation of the whole being. Being made right with God, through faith in Christ (the vertical relationship), enables us to be made right with our fellow man, through the power of Christ (the horizontal relationship). Christians are called to make a difference in their world.

WORLD IN NEED

The church in every generation has the duty to take the message of Christ into the marketplace. That task requires *determination* – that we may not be sidetracked from our main purpose. It requires *dedication* – that we might learn the skills as well as pay the price. Incarnation is a bloody, costly, messy business. It requires *translation* – the ability to communicate the unchanging message of the gospel in the language and thought-forms of today's people. Richard Baxter, a pastor in the middle of the great Civil War in England in the seventeenth century, wrote these challenging words:

> Be wise in using the apt expressions. Many a minister delivers a most excellent and useful matter in such harsh language that it makes the hearers loathe the food they should live by, and laugh at a sermon that might make them quake. So it is in private exhortation as well as public. If you clothe the most amicable truth in sordid language, you will make men disdain it as monstrous and deformed.
> (*The Saints Everlasting Rest* quoted in Sherwood Eliot Wirt *Exploring the Spiritual Life* ((Lion 1985) p 87)

The task of translation requires *love* – for without it we become, for all our zeal, a momentary distracting noise and no more (1 Cor 13:1). As Richard Baxter urged, 'Go to sinners with tears in your eyes.'

What is happening in today's marketplace? Not many engaged in evangelism would argue with Dr Billy Graham's assessment of the world scene, when he addressed an International Conference for Itinerant Evangelists in Amsterdam in 1983: 'There is an openness to the Gospel in this generation which we may never see again. Almost every book and newspaper screams from its pages; "The harvest is ripe".

'Seldom has the soil of the human heart and mind been better prepared. Never has the grain been thicker . . .' People are searching and, even in our materialistic, western society, that search continues, although not everybody would describe it in terms of a religious or spiritual quest. But all the signs are there if we are only willing to read them. Men and women are hungry for reality.

In certain parts of the world, the Christian church is experiencing remarkable growth. The *Evangelical Missions*

Quarterly for October 1979 reported a computerised survey conducted by The Centre for the Study of World Evangelization in Nairobi. The Centre had undertaken an in-depth analysis of the world scene. They claimed that in 1979 1.8 million professing Christians in Europe abandoned the faith whilst in North America the figure was almost one million. But, for the same period, the church in Africa had increased by six million and in South Asia the figure for those professing conversion was thirty-four million!

Even in the west, there are encouraging signs of hope. In recent years in Britain there have been positive indications that the tide has turned. The statistics of the 1984/5 Mission England project bear close study. Both attendances and response were far higher than anyone could have expected – if we were honest about our expectations. In the regional meetings held in six cities across England in 1984, 1,026,600 people attended with some 96,982 being counselled. With the 1985 meetings in Sheffield, the impact was even bigger, with a total attendance of 257,900 over the eight meetings with 26,131 making some form of public response. We British Christians are not famous for our optimism or faith, so the words of Billy Graham at the conclusion of his 1984 visit deserve careful pondering: 'There is no doubt that the three months during which I shared in Mission England were one of the highlights of my entire ministry' (Derek Williams *One in a Million* (Word Books 1985) p 187).

It would be all too easy to look back on the early years of the 1980s with such large-scale projects as Mission England and Mission to London and feel that we have discharged our responsibility. For all those reached through these evangelistic initiatives and the many localised events which they spawned, there remains a staggering forty-five million people in England and Wales who do not attend church on a regular basis, out of a total population approaching fifty million. That works out at 90% of the population. We have cause to be concerned about the size of the task before us. (See Peter

Brierley (ed) *Beyond the Churches* (MARC Europe Evangelical
Alliance 1984).)

There are thousands of unreached peoples on our doorstep
in Britain. The inner-cities, the large immigrant communities, the army of young people in our schools, colleges and
universities. The ordinary working-class man in the pub, the
media and the professional groups – nowhere can be allowed
to remain a 'No-go' area for the gospel of Jesus Christ.

CHURCH IN CHANGE

The Spirit of God has been blowing his winds of change
through the church in Britain. There are encouraging signs
of the evidence of his work. One of these signs is the way in
which evangelism has been moved further up the agenda for
many individual Christians and local churches.

In recent years, there have been five important areas
where this has been most noticeable:

A reappraisal of the meaning of evangelism

A division has arisen, since the turn of the century, between
those who advocated what became known as 'the social
gospel' and others, mainly on the evangelical wing of the
church, who maintained that this represented a betrayal of
the great commission which Jesus gave to preach, baptise,
teach and make disciples. Advocates of the social gospel
talked in terms of 'presence evangelism' – Christians must
earn the right to be heard, and their gospel must be seen in
acts of love, compassion and social righteousness. Unfortu-
nately those who advocated such an approach, often com-
bined it with a denial of basic biblical truths such as the
authority of the Bible, the person of Jesus and a denial of

some of the more miraculous elements of the gospel narrative.

Action always prompts reaction, and it would be fair to say that the evangelical community on the whole did not respond well to what many came to regard as a modern-day heresy. The pendulum swung too far the other way in reaction and, in John Stott's words, 'evangelicals concentrated on evangelism and philanthropy, and steered clear of socio-political action' (J R W Stott *Issues Facing Christians Today* (Marshalls 1984) p 8 John Stott – Marshalls). In rejecting the 'social gospel', evangelicals seemed to temporarily forget that the gospel must have a social dimension to it.

The Lausanne Congress on World Evangelization in 1974 bravely faced this area of neglect declaring that 'evangelism and socio-political involvement are both part of our Christian duty'. Following on from Lausanne, a special Consultation was convened in Grand Rapids, Michigan, USA, in 1982 which drew up an important report entitled *Evangelism and Social Responsibility*, which made an attempt to bridge an enormous gulf. It presented a synthesis of views from the worldwide Christian community; from those wrestling with the awful problems of poverty in the Third World to Christians coming to terms with liberation theology in the bloody revolutions of Latin America. It reached the important conclusion that social concern, social action and evangelism are inseparably bound together in the mission of the church. They are not competitors but, in reality, marriage partners.

A redefinition of the ministry of the evangelist

In recent years, the emergence of the study of what is known as Church Growth has produced many helpful insights. One of the trends noticed by Church Growth experts is that the average local church usually finds around 10% of its members have a special gift for evangelism. (That does not discharge the remaining 90% from the duties of Christian witness!) Following this through, local congregations of different denominations have begun to recognise and arrange specialist training for those with such gifts. The emphasis has been shifting away from the paid professional who is brought in to 'do' evangelism, to the more biblical approach of ordinary people learning how to give away their faith.

Dr Stuart Blanch, former Archbishop of York, reflected something of this redefinition when he spoke at the thanksgiving service for the life and ministry of David Watson, at York Minster in 1984, '. . . an evangelist is not necessarily a person with a striking style, not always a person with great charismatic gifts, but one who makes it easier for others to believe in God.'

A rediscovery of personal evangelism

One of the methods used by the first Christians was person-to-person evangelism. In many ways this is the ideal and most effective method of bringing people to Christ. It is wrong to be dogmatic, but perhaps the development of modern crusade evangelism in the late 1940s and early 1950s in Britain led the emphasis away from individual witness to the large-meeting concept.

In the 1970s Evangelism Explosion hit some British churches with enormous impact. This training scheme for personal evangelism originated out of the experience of a Presbyterian minister in Florida, USA. James Kennedy had pioneered a scheme of training his members to share their faith with confidence. Unashamedly using the best elements of sales techniques, hundreds of Christians found a new confidence in sharing the gospel. Soon, all over Britain, 'EE clinics', as they became known, drew together ministers and lay-leaders who were eager to learn. Relying heavily on one-to-one training, the scheme took root in many churches and the results were a powerful indication of its effectiveness. For example, one average-sized free church in the south of England reported 120 conversions over a six year period with the training of over 100 of its members in the EE technique of faith sharing.

A re-evaluation of mass evangelism

Although 'mass evangelism' has become a popular short-hand term within the Christian community, it is not a description that sits comfortably with most evangelists engaged in it. Perhaps a more acceptable description would be *large-scale evangelism*. It is, in other words, the use of large meetings (usually in a stadium or theatre) where an evangelist presents the Christian message, usually with an opportunity for those present to make a public response to the gospel by going forward at the conclusion of the meeting.

Billy Graham is the best known large-scale evangelist in the world, and certainly in the 2,000 year history of the Christian church, no preacher has reached so wide an audience. Since the major Billy Graham crusades in Britain from 1954–1966 a sceptical (I would add, cynical) attitude arose amongst some Christian leaders concerning the effectiveness of such an approach. The charges of emotionalism and mass-manipulation have often been laid at Billy Graham's door – with little or no evidence to support them. But perhaps the most serious criticism concerned the follow-up of those making some form of response at such meetings. Were they given sufficient aftercare to enable them to grow in their Christian commitment? Were they placed in churches where they could receive good, basic teaching? In other words, were 'decisions' translated into disciples?

Some of the criticisms had a valid basis and served to sharpen up training and follow-up methods for later missions such as Mission England and Mission to London (which was led by the Argentinian-born evangelist, Luis Palau). But the difference between 1966 and 1984 is almost twenty years, and during that period many changes have taken place in the British church. For one thing, there were hundreds of Christians who had never heard Billy Graham preach, or set foot in a large-scale evangelistic meeting. The vast majority of those who participated in the Mission England programme reported enthusiastically about its effect upon their own lives as well as on churches and surrounding communities.

Some remain unconvinced that large-scale meetings are the best way of reaching the unconverted. Others argue that – in the light of the enormity of the task – one of the best ways forward is to think big, and they point to the effective open-air preaching of Wesley and Whitefield in a previous generation as evidence of this.

Certainly there is a new-found confidence amongst British Christians concerning the gospel. Groups of churches in cities, towns and other areas are looking at ways in which to work effectively together in united evangelism. A large-scale project really does heighten the profile of the gospel and the prospect of Christians actually uniting to work together is surely no bad thing. For some it is the only valid form of true ecumenism – the coming together of Christians in the essentials of what they believe with a united concern for their community to understand the message of the good news of Jesus Christ.

In such situations, churches are encouragingly beginning to think British! There are many gifted evangelists in Britain, and some promising men and women among the younger generation. The late David Watson was the first British evangelist for some years to gain a truly international standing as a Christian preacher. Supremely he was an evangelist – who did much credit to that office by demonstrating powerfully that to be an evangelist meant more than preaching over and over again a handful of gospel sermons!

Some of the problems raised by those who are not happy with large-scale evangelism are, in my opinion, not so much theologically based as culturally based. The emergence of gifted British evangelists is enabling Christians to engage in large-scale evangelism within a cultural framework that is more acceptable and comfortable.

A renewal in many local churches

How do we gauge the spiritual state of the national church? Ultimately, the judgement that matters is left with God. But as the church in Britain is made up of many local churches of various shapes, sizes and shades, we gain some idea of our spiritual condition by beginning there.

Churches up and down the country report signs of renewal evidenced by a deepening of faith and personal commitment amongst Christians. Some churches speak of a deep work of the Holy Spirit in people's lives opening up new areas of worship, a deeper understanding of prayer and a more practical approach to fellowship. A renewed appreciation of the person, work and gifts of the Holy Spirit has come about in the past twenty years. Many believe that the age of miracles is far from over, and engage in regular prayers for the healing of the sick in body, mind and spirit during the course of services.

Not that all within the garden of the British churches is roses. Splits, hypocrisy, sensationalism and downright heresy all serve to show us that we still have an enemy who delights to sow weeds amongst God's flowers. Some, utterly preoccupied with getting the structures right have forgotten that even new wineskins have a limited lifespan and can rapidly become old.

Within spiritual renewal there must come a fresh examination of priorities. Prayer, worship, sacrificial giving, practical fellowship, social concern for the surrounding community, identification with other believers and renewed commitment to world mission are some of the priorities that have been emerging. Grouped among them – and, in some churches, head and shoulders above them – comes evangelism.

Any movement which claims to be of God and yet does not produce a heartfelt concern for those without Christ has a right to be challenged. Because God is a missionary he always seeks to reproduce within his children that same missionary heart. Any church that is undergoing renewal must face the challenge that the closer we come to God, the nearer he draws us to his world. In the memorable words of Elizabeth Goudge, 'if we go home like the Prodigal Son we must go out again as the Good Samaritan'.

The kingdom of darkness never feels threatened when we arrange a conference on evangelism, or if we decide to preach or write about it. That kingdom feels no danger when we pray about evangelism – if there is no real intention on our part to actually get involved. What the kingdom of darkness fears is when the Christian church takes seriously the command of her Lord to get involved in the costly work of evangelism and put it into practice – because the very gates of hell itself cannot withstand the powerful advance of God's kingdom.

Brother Andrew, writing in his book *Battle for Africa* tells a challenging story:

I have a young missionary friend, now a colleague of mine in Open Doors, who served for several years in Vietnam. He was at a conference of Christians in Da Nang shortly before it fell to the Communist armies. He told me that on that very day the Vietnamese pastors had spent the session discussing their 'Ten Year Plan' for Vietnam. It was business-as-usual – plans and projections – just as if the world were not exploding outside! They didn't have ten years. They didn't even have ten days! But they seemed oblivious to it. They vastly underestimated the power of

the Revolution, and while they should have been preparing the church to live under persecution, too many of them were talking about what buildings they should erect in the 1980s!
(Brother Andrew *Battle for Africa* (Marshalls 1978))

The kingdom of darkness has a weapon labelled 'distraction'. There are two sure defences against it – the word of God and prayer. Both sharpen our vision, build up our faith and lead us on from the place of being an onlooker. Instead of debating theories in our armchair we find ourselves in the thick of the battle and at the heart of God's purpose for his church.

4   A CALL TO COMMITMENT

'It is not weapons that decide the outcome of a war – but the men who carry the weapons.' So wrote Mao Tse-tung, revolutionary leader and founder of the People's Republic of China. Our success in evangelism depends totally upon God. But the level of our personal commitment is an important, determining factor.

Without the aid of mass-produced, high quality literature, sophisticated follow-up schemes, computerised record systems and hi-tech communications, the first Christians turned their world upside down. Lack of equipment is no great hindrance where faith and commitment abound.

WHAT SORT OF COMMITMENT?

We need to think about the shape that commitment must take:

A commitment to people

There is a well-known verse which runs:

> The kiss of the sun for pardon,
> The song of the birds for mirth,
> One is nearer God's heart in a garden
> Than anywhere else on earth.

Such sentiments (and sentiment is a good description for such an idea) are a nonsense which verge on the blasphemous. It is true that we can perceive much of the character of God from the beauty of the natural world that he has created. But to suggest that a flower brings us closer to his heart than a human being is to make the cross a sideshow attraction to the main event of creation. The Bible points us to the truth that we are nearer God's heart in the supermarket, on the football terraces, in a rush-hour train or amongst uniform rows of houses on a council estate. God's heartbeat is for men and women the world over – people matter to him. And people *must* matter to his people if we are truly to be about his business.

In the words of the great commission, Jesus tells us that going into the world to preach the gospel is an indispensable part of discipleship. Perhaps the thought of the world with its 4,000 million plus inhabitants divided into about 223 states and territories speaking 5,770 languages overwhelms us. But we each inhabit our individual 'world', made up of family, friends and the people whom we work alongside. That 'world' within the world needs to be invaded with the gospel of Jesus Christ, and God's human agent for doing that work is *you*. If each Christian in Britain led one other person to Christ the whole nation would be converted within four years!

Commitment to people takes up a great deal of time. It causes personal inconvenience and interrupts our private lives. People mess up the carpet, leave stains on the coffee-table and regularly forget to say 'thank you'. Incarnation – the word becoming flesh – involved God the Father, Son and Spirit in the same costly sacrifice of putting others before self. We need to ask God for a baptism of love, that, like Jesus, our hearts may be moved with compassion for shepherdless sheep (Matt 9:36–37).

A few years ago I was visiting a Muslim country which was fiercely opposed to the Christian gospel. There were just a handful of national believers who faced a tough time following Christ in their daily lives. I shared a bus journey with a

Christian from overseas who had come to live and work in
that country as an informal missionary. Knowing he had
spent some years working in this difficult situation and learnt
some hard lessons, I asked him what was really needed to see
a spiritual breakthrough amongst a people that were so
closed to the message of Jesus. His reply surprised me but I
have never forgotten it: '*miracles and martyrs*'. Miracles –
because people needed not only to hear the words of the good
news of Jesus, they needed to see the authority of Jesus
demonstrated in sick bodies and in those possessed by evil
spirits. Martyrs – because, in my friend's view, until people
saw Christians who loved them enough to die for them, they
would not believe in the message they preached. The words
of this mild, gentle Christian have remained with me, partly
because they did not come from an extrovert, powerful per-
sonality who might be expected to overstate his case. When
people see that we mean what we say they are more ready to
hear what we tell them. Actions and words belong together.

A commitment to prayer

Even the newest Christian believer will grasp that prayer is
an important part of growing as a disciple. We all know it is
important but it is its practice that creates the problems. We
may be stirred and challenged by a sermon or a book and
determine to do something to increase the effectiveness of our
prayer life only to find that, before long, we lapse back into
our hurried and selfish approach to God when we treat
prayer as a late-night dash to the supermarket to grab as
much as we can off the shelves before the doors close.

But praying for others – especially those who do not know
the Lord Jesus Christ – can revolutionise our whole attitude
to prayer. Sit down with a piece of paper and make a list of
those who inhabit your daily world and who are not committed Christians. Begin to pray for them regularly and speci-

fically – but watch out! Prayer is a dangerous weapon and we always need to be willing to become an answer to our own prayers on behalf of others.

The *Prayer Triplet Scheme*, initiated through Mission England was surely an inspired suggestion. The idea involves three Christians committing themselves to meet on a weekly basis to pray for three non-Christian friends each. Stories abound of hundreds of people coming to a personal faith in Jesus through such a simple, yet dedicated, act. For some, the prayer triplets have continued and, in certain churches, they have become part of the regular life of the congregation.

To enable individual Christians and churches to pray more effectively, the Evangelical Alliance launched an initiative in 1985 entitled '*A light in every street*' (see Appendix for details). The aim of the strategy is to see a Christian presence in every street, tower-block and village throughout Britain and, to that end, it seeks to encourage churches to use prayer triplets and neighbourhood Bible study groups to begin to pray regularly for every street in their area.

As helpful as a scheme may be, it depends on my commitment to take the matter of praying for others seriously. A close friend of mine was part of a triplet-group which had been praying for some of the mothers they met each day at the school gates. Months passed, and no great change was apparent in the three friends she prayed for. One morning, getting the children ready for school, she felt a distinct prompting from God to speak to one of these women. Taking her courage in both hands as they walked to school, she turned to her friend and blurted out, 'What would you say if I told you there was someone who loved you more than anyone else on earth ever can?' There was a stony silence and not a flicker of response. My friend gave up after a few mumbled sentences and retreated home confused about her guidance and convinced she had ruined a promising friendship. Later that day, a note came through the door from her school-gate contact explaining that she appreciated what was said and had not responded simply because she 'was too full up'. The note ended, 'But please, don't stop praying for me.' After several weeks, and a number of deep conversations, the lady in question came to a point of making a personal commitment to Jesus Christ. As events unravelled, it transpired that the night before their famous walk to school, which ended in embarrassed silence, the woman's husband had come home announcing that he believed their marriage was over and intended to file for divorce. After a sleepless night, racked with worries about an uncertain future and wrestling with personal guilt, the first person she met on the street asked the question, 'What would you say if I told you there was someone who loved you more than anyone else on earth ever can?'

With a story like that the pages of the New Testament spring to life, as we realise that the same Holy Spirit who prompted Philip to meet a royal official on a dusty desert road is able to move through our lives today if we are willing to pay the price of commitment in praying for others.

A commitment to involvement

Have you noticed how easy it is to leave the responsibility to the anonymous 'they'. 'They can do it' sums up our attitude so often when it comes to evangelism. We expect the church or its leaders to shoulder the task that is really ours.

John Stott wrote a book some years ago entitled *Our Guilty Silence*. Like Peter, warming himself by the fire, when challenged about being one of Christ's disciples, we opt out of our responsibility. John Stott commented: 'We should not lightly despise Peter, for we share his guilt too often. Indeed we are altogether too ready to find a scapegoat for our own guilty silence, and to blame everything and everybody except ourselves' (J R W Stott *Our Guilty Silence* (Hodder and Stoughton 1967) p 118).

But how do we become involved in evangelism if we find ourselves in an introverted church or amongst a group of Christians who are simply apathetic? The answer lies in two responses, *prayer* and *action*. We must pray for spiritual vision and we need to encourage it by being examples of what we pray for in others.

Involvement comes in many forms. Opening our homes for evangelistic Bible studies or supper parties, joining a secular club or society in order to build bridges of friendship with non-Christians, arranging outreach events amongst friends and colleagues or simply spending time sharing one-to-one with a neighbour.

Involvement means getting our hands dirty in serving others. It is no use handing an evangelistic tract to a person who cannot read or standing as a group of faithful witnesses on the corner of a council estate singing hymns and shouting the gospel from a soapbox while totally ignoring the needs of the people who live there.

Like the pendulum on a clock, we swing to extremes. Confronted with social deprivation some Christians have responded with the 'spiritual' answer – 'preach to them'! Others have responded with social concern – 'help them'! But both of these responses are bound up with bringing good news to people. The one does not exclude the other. The gospel of Jesus Christ is the only answer to the aching void in people's lives and we cannot hold back from presenting it as clearly as possible. But people need to see actions as well as hear words if they are going to understand the message properly.

Perhaps the greatest need for a particular area is a well-run playgroup for pre-school children, adult reading classes, a drop-in centre for young people, a community project for the unemployed, a 'good neighbour' scheme for the elderly. The list goes on. Involvement in evangelism means involvement with people. And that means involvement in their lives. As Christians we are called to preach *and bring* good news to people, wherever they are and whatever needs they may have.

In my work, which takes me all over Britain as well as to other parts of the world, I am constantly amazed at the creative ingenuity of the Holy Spirit at work in the lives of quite ordinary Christians. People who are willing to get involved, because their life ambition is to 'seek first his kingdom' (Matt 6:33).

A commitment to give

We meet it every time we see a campaigner for some political party or another, trudging through rain-drenched streets stuffing leaflets through letter boxes after a hard day at work. We see it in the single-minded dedication of the Olympic athlete working-out in the gym hours before most of us are out of bed. We find it in the lives of people who are sold out for a cause. In her biography, Winnie Mandela, wife of the jailed political leader Nelson Mandela, speaks of the total commitment of her marriage and family life to the fight for political change in South Africa: 'I am too small in this enormous liberation machine. Blacks are dying every day in this cause. Who am I to contribute my little life? The cause before us is too great for me to even be thinking of what happens to me personally' (Winnie Mandela *Part of my Soul* (Penguin 1985) p 14).

Giving obviously includes time, skills and energy. It also includes money. In our Christian giving, how much of it is specifically directed to world evangelism? Our true heart concern is always seen in the way we give of ourselves and our possessions.

A commitment to restructure

The problem in some of our churches is that we seek to *do* evangelism whilst failing to become evangelistic. Let me explain; it is one thing to make occasional attempts to reach those who are outside the Christian faith and quite another to structure the whole church programme around the primary goal of making disciples. Notice I used the words *making disciples*. Evangelism, in its fullest sense is not just proclaiming God's gift in Jesus but also teaching people what it means to live a Christian life, serving God effectively in the world.

In this sense all churches are to be evangelistic centres where we are engaged in a three-point strategy:

1) *Presenting* the gospel to those outside Christ;
2) *Teaching* the gospel to those who have committed themselves to Christ;
3) *Training* how to share the gospel with those outside Christ.

The objectives are:

1) To see people *becoming* disciples;
2) To see people *growing* as disciples;
3) To see people established in *reproducing* disciples.

This does not mean that pastoral care, fellowship life and other activities are minimised. They are important parts of growing in Christian maturity, but clear goals are needed if we are to fulfil God's purposes for his church.

In his book *I Believe in Evangelism* David Watson has written an incisive chapter on 'Evangelism and the local church' where he makes the telling point:

In many ways church missions and evangelistic crusades are God's second-best: if every local church were truly alive with the Spirit of God there would be no need for the considerable time, money and energy expended on these special events. Although the message of evangelism is

always Christ, the purpose and agent of evangelism is the Church.
(D Watson *I Believe in Evangelism* (Hodder and Stoughton 1976) p 134–5)

A commitment to planned action

Leadership is the key to moving a church forward, and unless leaders are motivated by God in their hearts they will not progress far. Planning is needed, once leaders have committed themselves to mobilise a congregation to on-going evangelism. Such planning is not unspiritual. Joshua issued the challenge to the tribes of Israel, 'How long will you wait before you begin to take possession of the land that the Lord, the God of your fathers, has given you?' (Joshua 18:3) Having stirred them in a sermon, Joshua set about organising them into action. Too often the challenge finishes in the pulpit and is never worked out in down-to-earth terms. Mobilisation of gifts and energies can include:

* **Prayer**	Enabling the congregation to pray in small groups, and encouraging schemes such as 'Light in every street'.
* **Teaching**	Creating a biblical awareness of the importance of evangelism.
* **Training**	Encouraging Christians to open their homes effectively, share their faith and use their gifts.
* **Target groups**	Focusing prayer and planning on specific unreached groups in the community, such as ethnic minorities, young people, men, etc.
* **Special services**	Learning to use the church programme and the Christian year for

	specific evangelistic services with clear preaching and a well-planned system of follow-up for interested contacts.
* Periods of mission	A concentrated period of special mission meetings, probably harnessing the gifts of others outside the local churches, designed to build lasting bridges into the local community.
* Developing evangelists	Discovering those amongst a congregation with special gifting in evangelism, and encouraging them to develop and train such a gift. (See Appendix for further details.)
* Community involvement	Establishing contacts within the community in schools, hospitals, factories, prisons, where regular opportunities can be used by teams from the church to visit and share their faith.
* Aftercare	Setting up nurture groups under trained leaders, to disciple and pastor new Christians. Organising Agnostics' Anonymous groups for those who have not made a Christian commitment but are wanting to think things through further.

JUGGLING WHILE ROME BURNS

You will have seen the juggling acts that occasionally appear on television. The part that always fascinates me is when the juggler balances plates on the end of bamboo poles by making them spin. Soon he has a whole line of spinning plates, precariously balanced. Then the fun begins. He runs up and down the line giving a frantic shake to a pole where the plate has almost stopped spinning before rushing on to the next and so on.

Some of us live our Christian lives like the juggler with his plates. Leaders can lead churches after the same fashion. Like balancing spinning plates, we suddenly notice that our involvement in evangelism is beginning to topple, so we rush to give the pole another shake.

The first Christians have much to teach us. As we face the last few remaining years of the twentieth century we need to learn four specific lessons from their example:

Clarity

We must be clear about the gospel of Jesus Christ. There is a need for us to be *faithful to the word*, not watering-down or reinterpreting the changeless truths. At the same time we are called to be *faithful to the world*. Archaic language, in-house jargon, man-made tradition and isolationism are betrayals of this responsibility. For some of us locked in the time warp of another era of church history, God holds us accountable for the lives of this generation. It is liberating to learn the lesson of history but slavery to hide in its shadow.

Urgency

I believe that a significant number of Christians are closet universalists. We believe, secretly, that everyone will make it in the end, that God (for all that's said about him) could never consign the ungodly to everlasting punishment and separation. Damnation is not digestible. As we examine the biblical basis of the good news we have to face the clear, if uncomfortable, truth that Jesus saw hell as a reality and defined his mission in terms of ransoming those who are perishing and seeking and saving the lost (John 3:16; Luke 19:10; Mark 10:45).

Faith

Without it we cannot please God (Heb 11:6). Without it we cannot effectively serve God. The first Christians faced a hostile world with a seemingly impossible mission. But believing in what is humanly unbelievable they moved forward in faith and obedience. Confronted with the needs of society today we may often feel overwhelmed. So it is the mustard seed principle we need always to keep before us (Matt 17:20).

Single-mindedness

Jesus, surrounded by pressing priorities, gave away the secret of his motivation: 'I have come down from heaven not to do my will but to do the will of him who sent me' (John 6:38). Go back to the synagogue at Nazareth where Jesus, in his first sermon, applied Isaiah's prophecy to himself, 'The Spirit of the Lord is on me, because he has anointed me to preach good news to the poor' (Luke 4:18). Literally translated it reads *'to evangelise the poor'*.

Evangelism for Jesus, and for us, is not just another plate needing an occasional shake to make it spin, but an essential part of God's purpose for our lives.

APPENDIX

For further reading:

Michael Green *Evangelism in the Early Church* (Highland Books 1984). A modern Christian classic. An indispensable textbook for anyone wanting to grasp the early church's theology and methods of evangelism.

David Watson *I Believe in Evangelism* (Hodder and Stoughton 1974). An important introduction to evangelism by one of Britain's finest preachers who knew first-hand about the subject from his own leadership of a local church and his experience as an international evangelist.

Clive Calver, Derek Copley, Bob Moffett and Jim Smith (eds) *A Guide to Evangelism* (Marshalls). A 'Yellow Pages' of evangelism packed with 300 pages of articles from seventy writers giving practical advice on almost every contemporary method in evangelism. Indispensable for leaders planning a strategy for the local church.

Rebecca Manley Pippert *Out of the Saltshaker* (IVP 1980). Sub-titled 'Evangelism as a Way of Life', this book takes the lid off the problems of personal faith-sharing. Honest, positive and practical advice for Christians wanting to bridge the communication gap.

For Further Information:

For details of '*Prayer Triplets*' and the '*Light in every street*' initiative please write to:

> Department of Evangelism
> Evangelical Alliance
> 186 Kennington Park Road
> LONDON SE11 4BT

The Evangelical Alliance is currently compiling a register of unreached people-groups to provide information and help to local churches; it is also in touch with evangelists, specialists in various spheres of outreach and agencies that exist to provide training for Christians in evangelism.